DEATH BY PET

A HILARIOUS HISTORY OF MISGUIDED HUMANS

DR. I.T. OLDUSO

ILLUSTRATIONS BY REBECCA PRY

CIDER MILL PRESS

BOOK PUBLISHERS

KENNEBUNKPORT, MAINE

MEET HARRY.

HIS PET
HIPPOPOTAMUS
KILLED HIM.

THE WEIGHT OF THE AVERAGE HUMAN IS ABOUT 140 LBS.

THE AVERAGE HIPPO WEIGHS IN AT AROUND 3,000 LBS.

ABOUT 1,000 LBS.
SHY OF AN SUV.

HARRY WAS NOT KILLED BY AN SUV, BUT IF HE WAS, IT WOULD LOOK LIKE THIS.

HIPPOS ARE VERY
DANGEROUS. ASK ANYBODY.

BUT THEY'RE ALSO ROUND
WITH STUMPY LEGS,
WHICH MAKES THEM CUTE.

CORGIS ARE ROUND WITH
STUMPY LEGS.

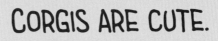

CORGIS ARE CUTE.

THE AVERAGE WEIGHT OF
A PEMBROKE WELSH CORGI
IS AROUND 25 LBS.

SIGNIFICANTLY LESS THAN EITHER A HIPPOPOTAMUS OR AN SUV.

THE BRITISH ROYAL FAMILY
HAS CORGIS.

SO FAR, THEY HAVEN'T BEEN
KILLED BY THEM.

LET'S REVIEW:

CORGI: 25 LBS.

HIPPOPOTAMUS:
ONE-AND-A-HALF TONS.

GO WITH THE CORGI.

THERE'S MONICA.

SHE HAS A CAT. LIKE DOGS, CATS BRING US GREAT JOY.

HOUSE CATS, THAT IS.

AS ANY CAT OWNER WILL
TELL YOU, HAVING A HOUSE CAT
ON YOUR LAP IS SO SATISFYING,
THAT YOU WILL DO ANYTHING
TO KEEP THEM THERE.

NOT SO WITH A TIGER.

AND YET, SOME PEOPLE THINK,
"I'M GOING TO GET A
PET TIGER."

NOW NORMAN DOESN'T
THINK ANYTHING.

HE'S DEAD.

MANY TIGERS LIVE
IN THE JUNGLE.

THE TIGER'S POWER HAS
BEEN IMMORTALIZED IN A
POEM BY WILLIAM BLAKE.

BUT WILLIAM BLAKE
WAS SMART ENOUGH NOT
TO OWN ONE.

A CAGE IS ABOUT AS FAR FROM

THE JUNGLE AS YOU CAN GET.

THERE'S A POSSIBILITY THAT A PET TIGER MIGHT, AT SOME POINT, THINK YOUR HOUSE IS A JUNGLE.

SHOULD THAT OCCUR,

THIS IS WHAT HAPPENS.

THE LION IS
THE KING OF THE BEASTS.

VICTOR WAS NOT
THE KING OF ANYTHING.

VICTOR WAS KILLED
BY HIS PET LION.

THE LIST OF
DEATH BY PET
GOES ON.

WANT TO SEE
SOME MORE OF
THE LIST?

YOU KNOW YOU
WANT TO SEE SOME MORE
OF THE LIST.

HERE YOU GO, YOU SICKO.

HERE'S SOMEONE
WHO KEPT A PET CAMEL
THAT TRIED TO MATE
WITH THEM.

YOU COULD SAY THIS
PERSON WAS HUMPED
TO DEATH.

(SORRY. COULDN'T RESIST.)

RORY WAS ASPHYXIATED BY HIS PET PYTHON.

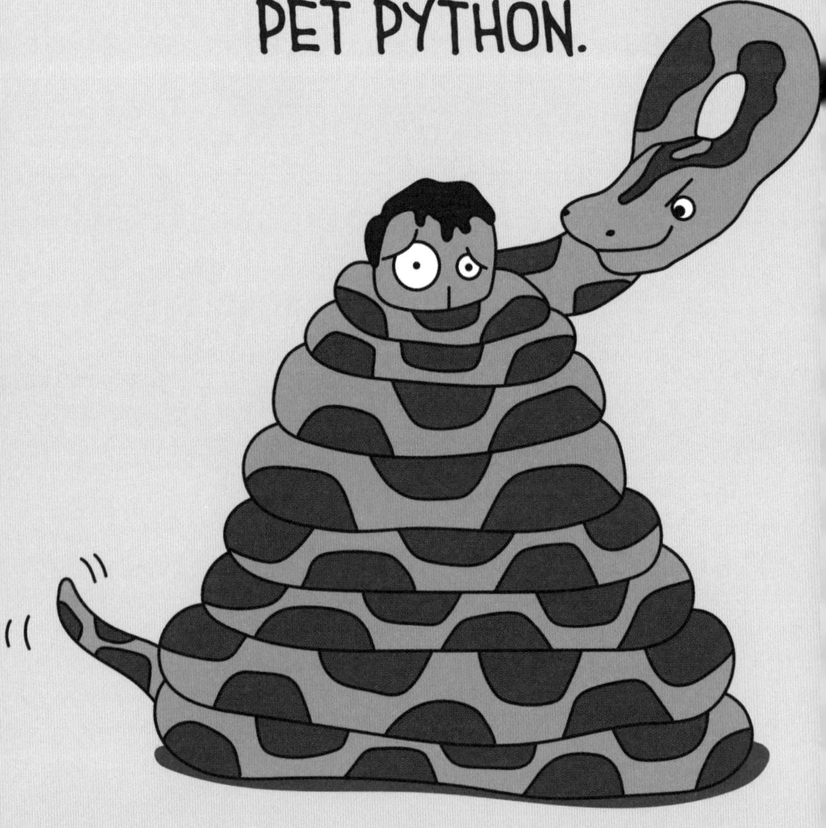

OUR INTERN WYATT
LOOKED UP "PYTHON" IN
THE DICTIONARY, WHEREIN IT
STATES THAT PYTHONS KILL
BY ASPHYXIATION.

UP TO THAT POINT, WYATT WAS ACTUALLY THINKING OF GETTING HIMSELF A PET PYTHON, BUT HE WILL NOT BE DOING THAT NOW.

WYATT DOES NOT
WANT TO BE ASPHYXIATED,
YOU SEE.

SO, WHEN YOU THINK "HOUSE PET," DON'T THINK A SNAKE THAT CAN STRANGLE YOU.

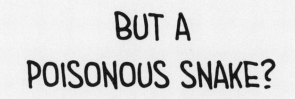

BUT A
POISONOUS SNAKE?

WHY THE HELL NOT?

HERE'S STACEY.

STACEY'S DEAD.
HER HIGHLY VENOMOUS
PET VIPER BIT HER.

AND THEN
THERE WAS
THE DUDE WHO
KEPT A PET
BLACK WIDOW
SPIDER.

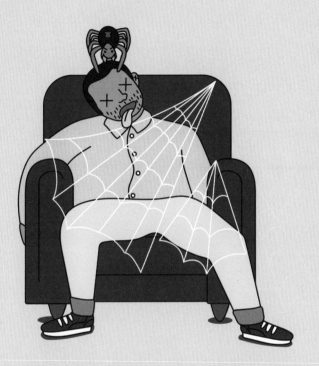

WAY AHEAD OF US, I SEE.

THERE ARE DOGS
THAT ARE ALMOST AS
TINY AS A SPIDER.

THERE ARE DOGS THAT ARE COMPARABLE IN SIZE TO A TIGER.

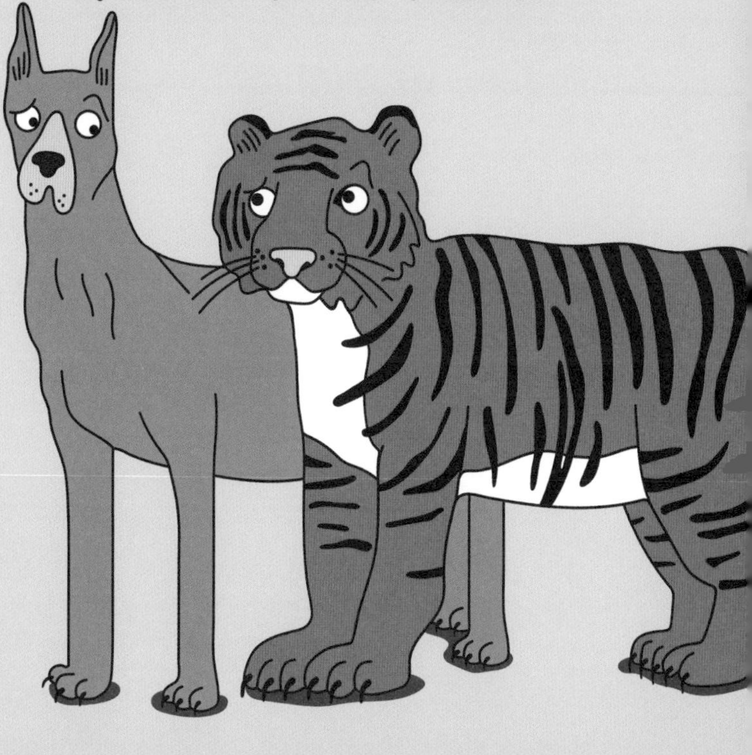

HOWEVER, DOGS' ATTEMPTS
TO HUMP YOU ARE CONFINED
TO YOUR LEG.

THEY ARE INCAPABLE OF
STRANGLING YOU.

AND THE ONLY
POISONOUS THINGS
ABOUT THEM ARE
THEIR FARTS.

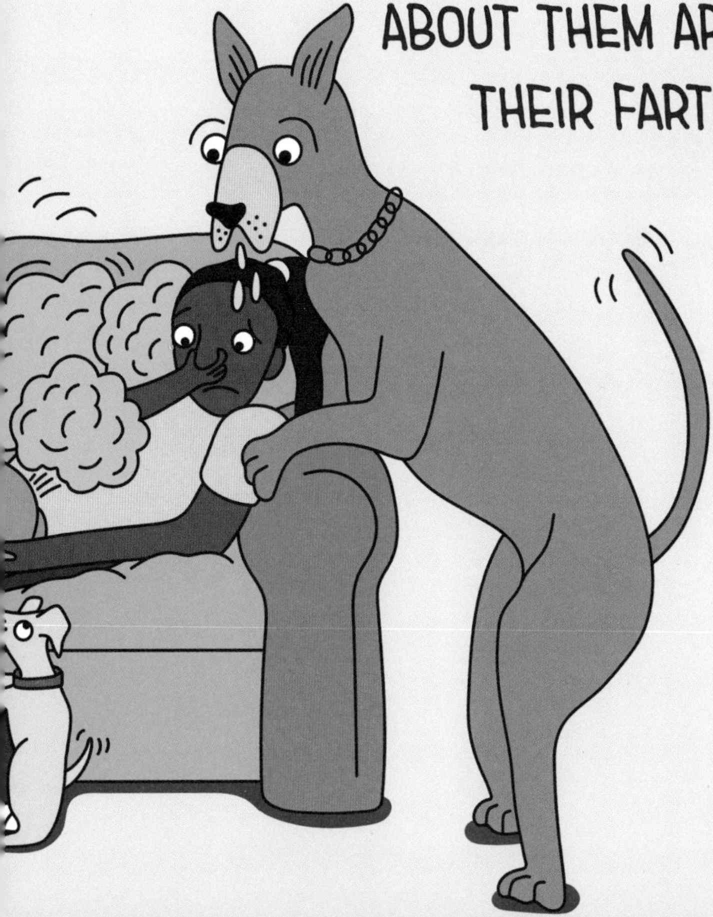

THIS LADY KEPT A PET BEAR IN A CAGE.

IT DIDN'T GO WELL.

BUT YOU KNEW THAT.

A LOT OF PEOPLE SEEM TO
DIG MACAQUE MONKEYS.

MACAQUE MONKEYS REALLY ENJOY BITING THE LIVING CRAP OUT OF PEOPLE.

WILD ANIMALS GOTTA BE WILD ANIMALS.

DON'T BE BLAMING THEM.

VETERINARIANS AND THOSE EXPERTS FROM DEPARTMENTS OF HEALTH AND DISEASE CONTROL SAY EXOTIC ANIMALS ARE DIFFICULT TO CONTROL AND ARE OFTEN ABANDONED BY THEIR OWNERS.

ALSO, FOR A VARIETY OF HEALTH AND SAFETY REASONS, THESE EXPERTS ADVISE AGAINST KEEPING EXOTIC ANIMALS AS PETS.

SO, IF ANYONE'S
TO BLAME, IT'S THESE
SO-CALLED EXPERTS.

JUST KIDDING.

IT'S US.

SOME CELEBRITIES HAVE

OWNED WILD ANIMALS.

BABOU NEVER
KILLED DALI.

MAYBE THE DUDE WAS
JUST TOO WEIRD.

ELVIS HAD A PET CHIMPANZEE NAMED SCATTER.

MICHAEL JACKSON
HAD BUBBLES.

SCATTER AND BUBBLES
DID NOT KILL ELVIS
OR MICHAEL.

FAME DID.

SO FAR, WILD ANIMALS
REMAIN UNTOUCHED BY
THE PRESSURES OF FAME.

IF ONLY THEIR
HOUSE PET COUSINS
HAD IT SO GOOD.

HUMANS WILL DO
ANYTHING TO GET PEOPLE TO
WATCH THEIR INTERNET VIDEOS.

TO THE POINT WHERE MANY OF
THEM THINK A SELFIE WITH A
WILD ANIMAL IS A GOOD IDEA.

HERE'S ZOE, A POPULAR
INSTAGRAM MODEL.

SHE THOUGHT IT WOULD BE FUN TO POSE WITH SOME NURSE SHARKS.

DON'T WORRY, SHE'S ALIVE.

THESE EXAMPLES OF
QUESTIONABLE HUMAN
INTELLIGENCE ARE
REPRESENTATIVE OF SO
MANY OTHERS WHO TRY
TO GET AS CLOSE
TO GRIZZLY BEARS
AS POSSIBLE.

CLEARLY, WILD THINGS HAVE A CERTAIN APPEAL TO US DOMESTICATED HUMANS.

BUT WHY DO
SOME OF US TAKE
IT TOO FAR?

LIKE THAT GUY WHO
WENT TO LIVE AMONG
THE GRIZZLIES.

HE STAYED A LITTLE
TOO LATE INTO FOOD-
GATHERING SEASON AND
BECAME THE FOOD.

OR THE FELLOW WHO
HAD A SWEET DEAL BREEDING
CASSOWARIES.

THING IS . . . CASSOWARIES
ARE WIDELY CONSIDERED TO BE
THE MOST DANGEROUS BIRDS
ON THE PLANET.

WITH ONE SWIFT KICK,
THEIR CLAWS CAN SLICE
OPEN A PREDATOR.

OR, YOU KNOW, A PERSON
WHO BREEDS THEM.

WHICHEVER COMES FIRST.

SPEAKING OF LARGE,
FLIGHTLESS BIRDS. YOU'VE
HEARD OF EMUS, RIGHT?

IT WAS IN AUSTRALIA, IN 1932. THE EMUS WEREN'T EVEN KILLING ANYBODY. THEY WERE JUST GOING NUTS, DESTROYING FARMERS' CROPS.

SO THE GOVERNMENT BROUGHT IN THE MILITARY TO MOW THEM DOWN WITH MACHINE GUNS. IT WAS DUBBED "THE EMU WAR."

AN EMU KICK CAN BE LETHAL, AND AS FAR AS THE DAMAGE ITS CLAWS CAN DO, CAN YOU SAY "CASSOWARY?"

NO, SERIOUSLY, CAN YOU?
IT'S NOT AN EASY WORD, CASSOWARY.

ANYWAY, POINT IS, THESE BADASS BIRDS STOOD UP TO MACHINE GUN FIRE AND DID NOT RELENT.

AND YET, SOME PEOPLE INSIST ON KEEPING THEM AS EXOTIC PETS.

LIKE ARNIE, HERE.

BEST OF LUCK TO YOU, ARNIE!

SO, YEAH,
WHEN THINKING
ABOUT ADDING A
PET TO YOUR HOME,
STICK WITH THE
CLASSICS.

THEY MAY RUIN
YOUR FURNITURE.

OR EAT YOUR
TV REMOTE.

BUT THEY WON'T
EAT YOU.

UNLESS THEY'RE REALLY, REALLY, REALLY, REALLY, REALLY, REALLY HUNGRY.

DEATH BY PET

This book may be ordered by mail from the publisher. Please include $5.99 for postage and handling. Please support your local bookseller first!

Books published by Cider Mill Press Book Publishers are available at special discounts for bulk purchases in the United States by corporations, institutions, and other organizations. For more information, please contact the publisher.

Cider Mill Press Book Publishers
"Where good books are ready for press"
PO Box 454
12 Spring Street
Kennebunkport, Maine 04046

Visit us online!
cidermillpress.com

Typography: Archer, ImaginaryFriend BB

Printed in China
1 2 3 4 5 6 7 8 9 0

First Edition

ABOUT CIDER MILL PRESS BOOK PUBLISHERS

Good ideas ripen with time. From seed to harvest, Cider Mill Press brings fine reading, information, and entertainment together between the covers of its creatively crafted books. Our Cider Mill bears fruit twice a year, publishing a new crop of titles each spring and fall.

Cider Mill Press Book Publishers
"Where good books are ready for press"
12 Spring Street | PO Box 454
Kennebunkport, Maine 04046
Visit us online! cidermillpress.com